A Paines Plough and Rose Theatre production,
in association wi

A SUDDEN VIOLENT BURST OF RAIN

by Sami Ibrahim

A Sudden Violent Burst of Rain

by Sami Ibrahim

Cast

NARRATOR 1/LANDOWNER'S SON/ GATEKEEPER/WORKER	Samuel Tracy
NARRATOR 2/LANDOWNER/LILY/ REGISTRAR'S REGISTRAR'S ASSISTANT/WOMAN	Princess Khumalo
NARRATOR 3/ELIF/GRAN	Sara Hazemi

Production Team

Director	Yasmin Hafesji
Design	Ryan Dawson Laight
Composer and Sound Designer	Roly Botha
Casting Director	Annelie Powell CDG
Lighting	Rory Beaton
Lighting Programmer and Lighting Associate	Jack Ryan
Movement	Yami Löfvenberg
Assistant Director	Joelle Ikwa
Company Stage Manager	Verity Clayton
Deputy Stage Manager	Charlotte Smith-Barker
Production Manager	Guy Ongley
Touring Technician	Zak Brewin
Touring Technician	Jack Scanlon

SAMI IBRAHIM (Writer)
Theatre includes: *two Palestinians go dogging* (Royal Court/Theatre Uncut); *Metamorphoses* (Shakespeare's Globe); *50 Berkeley Square* (Deep Night, Dark Night/Shakespeare's Globe); *Wonder Winterland* (Oxford School of Drama/Soho Theatre); *the Palestinian in the basement is on fire* (Pint-Sized/The Bunker); *Wind Bit Bitter, Bit Bit Bit Her* (VAULT Festival); *Iron Dome Fog Dome* (The Yard/First Drafts); *Carnivore* (Write Now 7 Festival/Brockley Jack). Audio includes: *The Twig* (That Podcast/ ETT); *Fledgling* (Radio 4). He won Theatre Uncut's Political Playwriting Award for *two Palestinians go dogging* and has been a writer-in-residence at Shakespeare's Globe as well as part of the Genesis/Almeida New Playwrights scheme. He has been on attachment at the National Theatre Studio and Theatr Clwyd, as well as a member of the Tamasha Writers Group and Oxford Playhouse Playmaker programme.

YASMIN HAFESJI (Director)
Theatre includes: *The Maladies* (Almeida Young Company/Yard Theatre); *Kick* (Lyric Hammersmith Studio, Bill Cashmore Award winner); *The Letters Project* (Gate Theatre Online, Co-Director); *George* (Gate Theatre Online); *Rhinoceros* (Lyric Evolution Festival, Lyric Hammersmith); *Rashida* (Fresh Direction/Young Vic Directors Program/Young Vic/Maria); *Two Heads and a Hand* and *The Jokers* (Shubbak Festival/Gate Theatre); *Watch Me Dance!* (White City Youth Theatre Summer Project/Bush Theatre); *Young Writers Group Showcase* (Bush Theatre Studio). Assistant Director credits include: *The Tragedy of Macbeth* (Almeida Theatre); *Women Beware Women* (Shakespeare's Globe); *Fairview* (Young Vic Theatre); *Dear Elizabeth* (Gate Theatre); *The Mob Reformers* (Lyric Hammersmith). She is Associate Director at the Gate Theatre and was a member of the Young Vic Introduction to Directing Programme 2017, led by Natalie Abrahami. As a

freelance director Yasmin has directed new plays, reimagined classics, and youth theatre across London.

SAMUEL TRACY (Narrator 1 / Landowner's Son / Gatekeeper / Worker)
Samuel Tracy is a recent graduate of The Royal Academy of Dramatic Art. They also trained at The BRIT School receiving qualifications in Theatre and Dance. Samuel is also a Deviser/Theatremaker and won the Strawberry Picking New Writing Best Play Award for *Branches, Twigs and Synapses*. Theatre includes: *Romeo and Juliet, Sticky* (Southwark Playhouse); *Dr. Jekyll & Mr Hyde* (Rose Theatre); *Zigger Zagger* (Wilton's Music Hall); *Orfeo* (Royal Opera House/Roundhouse). Television includes: *Woke Overnight* (BBC).

PRINCESS KHUMALO (Narrator 2 / Landowner / Lily / Registrar's Registrar's Assistant / Woman)
Princess Khumalo is a Zimbabwean-born actor who graduated from LIPA in 2021. Princess is very excited to be a part of Paines Plough Roundabout rep season. She has featured in CBBC's *So Awkward*. Since graduating from LIPA, Princess has starred in BBC's *Doctors* and also filmed a lead part in a UK TV comedy pilot, *Holier Than Thou*, which is set to be aired on DAVE this summer. Princess has also been lucky enough to have toured the north with various Liverpool production companies including All Things Considered Theatre Company, Out The Attic Theatre Company and Falling Doors Theatre in collaboration with Everyman and Playhouse Theatre.

SARA HAZEMI (Narrator 3 / Elif / Gran)
Sara Hazemi is a British-Iranian actor and writer from London. She is thrilled to be a part of this year's Roundabout season, and to share these stories with audiences across the UK. Theatre credits include: *Tales*

from *Hans Christian Andersen* (Guildford Shakespeare Company); *A Midsummer Night's Dream* (Guildford Shakespeare Company); *The Little Mermaid* (Fever); *Oedipus at Colonus* (Cambridge Arts Theatre); *Othello* (European Theatre tour); *A Series of Improvable Events* (The Cambridge Impronauts/Edinburgh Fringe/Gilded Balloon). Television credits include *This Is Going to Hurt* (BBC); *The Cockfields* (Gold).

RYAN DAWSON LAIGHT (Designer)
Theatre includes: *My Son's a Queer But What Can You Do, Torch Song* (Turbine Theatre); *My Brilliant Friend* (National Theatre, Associate Costume Design for Soutra Gilmore); *Pinocchio, The Wizard of Oz, Crossing Lines, Sleeping Beauty, Beauty and the Beast, Peter Pan, A Christmas Carol, Grimm Tales, The Tiger Who Came To Tea* (all for Chichester Festival Theatre). As Associate Designer at Creation Theatre, recent work includes: *Grimm Tales, Alice: A Digital Wonderland, Don Quixote, The Tempest, The Snow Queen, Peter Pan, Brave New World, Swallows and Amazons, Dracula, A Christmas Carol, Alice in Wonderland, Hamlet, Macbeth, As You Like It, Henry IV, King Lear* and *Treasure Island*. For Le Gateau Chocolat: *Duckie* (Royal Festival Hall); *Icons* (Edinburgh Festival); *Black* (Unity Theatre Liverpool/Soho Theatre); *Le Gateau Chocolat* (Menier Chocolate Factory); *HMS Pinafore, Chess, Blondel* and *The Mikado* (Union Theatre national tours); for the Brit School: *Landmines* (Ovalhouse); *Sticky and Infinite Joy* (Southwark Playhouse); *Chip Shop The Musical* (Octagon Theatre Bolton); *Ice Cream Opera* (Freedom Arts Studio). Dance includes: *Botis Seva's BLKDOG* (Sadler's Wells, Olivier Award Best New Dance 2019); *Blak Whyte Gray* (Boy Blue/Barbican, Olivier Award Nomination 2018); *REDD* (Boy Blue/Barbican Theatre); *Madhead* (NYDC/Sadler's Wells); *Wasteland, Coal* (Gary Clark Company, UK Theatre Award for Achievement in Dance); *Toro, Mariposa, Ham and Passion* (DeNada Dance Theatre); *Drew*

McOnie's Drunk (Leicester Curve/ Bridewell Theatre); *Good Morning Midnight* (Jermyn Street Theatre); *Genius* (Anjali); *New Ways of Living* (Pink Fringe Brighton); *Je Suis* (Aakash Odedra Company/Lillian Baylis Studio, Sadler's Wells); *Ruffle* (Carlos Pons Guerra/Rambert Dance/Lowry Theatre); *Hear Hear* (Deaf Men Dancing/Sadler's Wells).

ROLY BOTHA (Composer and Sound Designer)
Roly is a composer and sound designer and they're proud to be an Associate Artist of The PappyShow. Theatre includes: *Coming to England* (Birmingham Rep); *Orlando* (Jermyn Street); *WILD* (Unicorn); *Muck* (Park Theatre); *Blowhole* (Soho Theatre); *Milk & Gall* (Theatre503); *Fritz & Matlock* (Pleasance London/ Edinburgh Fringe Festival/Pleasance Edinburgh); *Helen* (BAC); *Brother* (Southwark Playhouse); *Warheads* (Park Theatre – 2020 Olivier nominated); *BOYS, GIRLS, CARE* (The PappyShow/national tour); and *Making Fatiha* (Camden People's Theatre). Audio includes: *It's a Practice Podcast* (The PappyShow); *Plays for Today* (Southwark Playhouse). Trans people, especially black trans femmes, are being discriminated against more than ever. Please consider donating to the charities Gendered Intelligence or Not A Phase.

ANNELIE POWELL CDG (Casting Director)
Theatre credits include: *House of Shades, Vassa* (Almeida); *Coming to England, What's New Pussycat?* (Birmingham Rep); *Wendy and Peter Pan* (Leeds Playhouse), as well as recent work for Hampstead Theatre, Hull Truck Theatres, Hoxton Hall, Theatr Clwyd, Headlong, Royal and Derngate Northampton, English Touring Theatre and The Bush Theatre. For Nuffield Southampton Theatres as Head of Casting credits include: *The Audience, Billionaire Boy, The Shadow Factory, Don Carlos, Fantastic Mr Fox, A Streetcar Named*

Desire (Nuffield Southampton Theatres/Theatr Clwyd/English Touring Theatre). For the Royal Shakespeare Company credits include: *Hamlet, King Lear, Imperium, Myth, The Rover, Seven Acts of Mercy, Two Noble Kinsman, Wendy and Peter Pan, Oppenheimer* (RSC/West End – Co Casting). Annelie's television work includes projects with Netflix, Apple, Warner Brothers, BBC, ITV and Nickelodeon alongside her work on Independent Feature Films and Adverts.

RORY BEATON (Lighting Designer)
Rory is a freelance lighting designer working both in the UK and internationally. He has previously been nominated for a Knight of Illumination Award for his work on *Così fan Tutte* at Opera Holland Park. He is also a recipient of the Michael Northen Award, presented by the Association of Lighting Designers. Previous projects include: *For Black Boys Who Have Considered Suicide When The Hue Gets Too Heavy* (Royal Court); *I Love You, You're Perfect, Now Change* (London Coliseum/Broadway HD); *Lovely Ugly City* (Almeida); *Spike, Kiss Me Kate* (Watermill); *Dishoom!* (UK tour); *Summer Holiday, The Rise and Fall of Little Voice* (Bolton Octagon); *Edward II* (West End); *Macbeth, La Bohème, Elizabeth I, The Marriage of Figaro, Dido & Aeneas, Amadigi, Il Tabarro, Idomeneo, Radamisto* (English Touring Opera); *West End Producer - Free Willy!* (Cuffe & Taylor); *60 Miles by Road or Rail* (Theatre Royal Northampton); *Tumble Tuck* (King's Head); *The Blonde Bombshells of 1943, Summer Holiday, A Christmas Carol* (Pitlochry); *How Love is Spelt* (Southwark Playhouse); *Skylight, The Mountaintop* (Chipping Norton/tour); *Maklena* (tour); *70 Års Opera* (Danish National Opera); *A Christmas Carol* (Belgrade/Chipping Norton); *Little Women, L'amico Fritz, The Cunning Little Vixen, Così fan Tutte, L'arlesiana, Manon Lescaut, Le Nozze di Figaro* (Opera Holland Park); *Dubliners* (OTC Ireland); *Mad Man Sad Woman* (Head for Heights). Rory has also designed

projects with Blenheim Palace and The British Library.
www.rorybeaton.co.uk

JACK RYAN (Lighting Programmer and Lighting Associate)
Jack is a freelance Lighting Programmer, Designer and Associate working both in the UK and internationally. His credits as lighting programmer include: *Choir of Man* (West End); *Macbeth, Elizabeth I, Idomeneo, Amadigi, Dido and Aeneas, Jonas, Radamisto* (English Touring Opera); *Christmas @ Blenheim Palace* (Sony/Culture Creative) as well as companies including: Crossroads Entertainment, Selladoor, Immersion Theatrical and Rambert Dance Company. Jack also works in live broadcast and commercials including work for companies such as: Peloton, Samsung, EA Sports and Vanish. Previous design credits include projects for Smyle with companies such as BMW, Samsung and Abbey Road Studios (artists incl. AlunaGeorge and Gavin DeGraw); *Blood Upon the Rose* (Hammersmith Apollo, SEC Armadillo, The Gaiety Theatre) and regularly designs a range of performances at Union Chapel, Islington. Jack is also the Associate Lighting Designer for the West End production of *Choir of Man*. Jack has also worked with artists such as Becky Hill, Celeste, Nao and Laura Mvula.

YAMI LÖFVENBERG (Movement Director)
Yami Löfvenberg is a movement director, theatre director and a multidisciplinary artist working in the intersection of movement, theatre and cross-arts. Between making her own work, Yami mentors educate and deliver workshops nationally and internationally. She is currently the lecturer on the first-ever Hip-Hop module at Trinity Laban Dance Conservatoire. A British Council and Arts Council England recipient, Howard Davies Emerging Directors Grant recipient, One Dance UK DAD

Trailblazer Fellow, Marion North Recipient, and a Talawa Make Artist. She was on the creative choreographic team for the 2012 Olympics Opening Ceremony and is a member of performance collective Hot Brown Honey. Movement Director credits include; *The Concrete Jungle Book* (Pleasance); *Kabul Goes Pop* (Brixton House); *Human Nurture* (Theatre Centre/Sheffield Theatre); *Athena* (The Yard); *Notes on Grief* (Manchester International Festival); *Rare Earth Mettle*, *Living Newspaper* (Royal Court); *Fuck You Pay Me* (Bunker); *Breakin' Convention* (Sadler's Wells); *Talawa TYPT* (Hackney Showrooms); *Boat* (BAC). Director credits include: *Fierce Flow* (Hippodrome Birmingham); *Kind of Woman* (Camden People's); *Afroabelhas* (Roundhouse/British Council/Tempo Festival (Brazil). Assistant Director/Choreographer credits include: *Hive City Legacy* (Roundhouse, Home, Millennium).

JOELLE IKWA (Assistant Director)
Joelle Ikwa is an aspiring Director and is delighted to be working as a Trainee Director with Paines Plough, as part of her three-month placement with RTYDS. Joelle is assisting all three plays for the Roundabout 2022 season. Her journey began in Coventry at the Belgrade Theatre over 10 years ago, where she went from a youth company member, workshop facilitator, assistant director to director. Joelle wants to share stories that empower and make a difference. With experience as a youth violence intervention worker, Joelle is passionate about raising awareness around issues that affect young people such as knife crime and mental health. Theatre being Joelle's creative conduit, she finds fulfilment in the positive impact that it has on people. Touring through the placement on Roundabout will add to Joelle's knowledge as she's burgeoning in this journey. Acting credits include: *The Tempest* (Belgrade Theatre); *Coventry Moves* (City of Culture). Assistant

Director credits include: *This Little Relic* (BBC); *Nothello* (Belgrade Theatre). Director credits include: *Transcend* (Bramall Music Hall).

VERITY CLAYTON (Company Stage Manager)
Verity has worked in theatres across the UK and abroad – mooring her narrowboat nearby when possible! Theatre includes: *Sorry You're Not a Winner* (Paines Plough/Theatre Royal Plymouth); *The Storm Whale* (York Theatre Royal/The Marlowe); *The Snail and the Whale* (Tall Stories/West End/ Sydney Opera House); *Alice and the Little Prince* (Pleasance, Edinburgh/ Lyric Hammersmith); *The Journey Home* (Little Angel/Beijing), *There's a Rang Tan in my Bedroom*, *The Singing Mermaid* and *WOW! Said the Owl* (Little Angel); *Under the Rainbow* (Polka Theatre/Galway & Wilderness Festivals); *Recycled Rubbish* (Theatre Rites).

CHARLOTTE SMITH-BARKER (Assistant Stage Manager)
Charlotte studied English Literature and Film at Aberystwyth University and Malmo University in Sweden. Upon graduating in 2018, she completed the Association of British Theatre Technicians' Bronze Award. When not working in theatre, Charlotte teaches English as a foreign language. Theatre includes: *The Catherine Tate Show* (West End); *Clybourne Park* (Park Theatre); *Soho Cinders* (Charing Cross Theatre); *The Sweet Science of Bruising* (Wilton's Music Hall).

 **Paines Plough**

Paines Plough is a touring theatre company dedicated entirely to developing and producing exceptional new writing. The work we create connects with artists and communities across the UK.

'The lifeblood of the UK's theatre ecosystem' *Guardian*

Since 1974 Paines Plough has worked with over 300 outstanding British playwrights including James Graham, Sarah Kane, Dennis Kelly, Mike Bartlett, Sam Steiner, Elinor Cook, Vinay Patel, Zia Ahmed and Kae Tempest.

'That noble company Paines Plough, de facto national theatre of new writing' *Daily Telegraph*

Furthering our reach beyond theatre walls our audio app COME TO WHERE I'M FROM hosts 180 original mini plays about home and our digital projects connect with audiences via WhatsApp, phone, email and even by post.

Wherever you are, you can experience a Paines Plough Production.

'I think some theatre just saved my life' @kate_clement on Twitter

PAINES PLOUGH · ROUNDABOUT

'A beautifully designed masterpiece in engineering' *The Stage*

ROUNDABOUT is Paines Plough's beautiful portable in-the-round theatre. It's a completely self-contained 168-seat auditorium that flat packs into a single lorry and pops up anywhere from theatres to school halls, sports centres, warehouses, car parks and fields.

We built ROUNDABOUT to tour to places that don't have theatres. ROUNDABOUT travels the length and breadth of the UK bringing the nation's best playwrights and a thrilling theatrical experience to audiences everywhere.

ROUNDABOUT was designed by Lucy Osborne and Emma Chapman at Studio Three Sixty in collaboration with Charcoalblue and Howard Eaton.

WINNER of Theatre Building of the Year at The Stage Awards 2014

'ROUNDABOUT wins most beautiful interior venue by far @edfringe.'
@ChaoticKirsty on Twitter

'ROUNDABOUT is a beautiful, magical space. Hidden tech make it Turkish-bath-tranquil but with circus-tent-cheek. Aces.'
@evenicol on Twitter

ROUNDABOUT was made possible thanks to the belief and generous support of the following Trusts and individuals and all who named a seat in Roundabout. We thank them all.

TRUSTS AND FOUNDATIONS
Andrew Lloyd Webber Foundation
Paul Hamlyn Foundation
Garfield Weston Foundation
J Paul Getty Jnr Charitable Trust
John Ellerman Foundation

CORPORATE
Universal Consolidated Group
Howard Eaton Lighting Ltd
Charcoalblue
Avolites Ltd
Factory Settings
Total Solutions

Roundabout is supported by the Theatres Trust in 2021.

Pop your name on a seat and help us pop-up around the UK:
https://www.justgiving.com/fundraising/roundaboutauditorium

Paines Plough

Joint Artistic Directors and CEOs	Charlotte Bennett & Katie Posner
Associate Artistic Director	Jesse Jones
Interim Executive Producer	Ellie Claughton
Incoming Executive Director	Jodie Gilliam
Producer	Lauren Hamilton
Outgoing Producer	Tanya Agarwal
Incoming Producer	Ellie Fitz-Gerald
Digital Producer	Nick Virk
Marketing and Audience Development Manager	Manwah Siu
Assistant Producer	Ellen Larson
Assistant Producer	Gabi Spiro
Administrator	Katie Austin
The Big Room Playwright Fellow	Mufaro Makubika
Press Representative	Bread & Butter PR

Board of Directors

Ankur Bahl, Corey Campbell, Kim Grant (Chair), Asma Hussain, Tarek Iskander, Olivier Pierre-Noël, Carolyn Saunders, Laura Wade.

Paines Plough Limited is a company limited by guarantee and a registered charity. Registered Company no: 1165130

Paines Plough, 38 Mayton Street, London, N7 6QR

office@painesplough.com
www.painesplough.com

 Follow @PainesPlough on Twitter

 Like Paines Plough at facebook.com/PainesPloughHQ

 Follow @painesplough on Instagram

Donate to Paines Plough at justgiving.com/PainesPlough

(ANTI)EST.1979
GATE
theatre

'London's most relentlessly ambitious theatre' *Time Out*

The Gate Theatre was founded in 1979 to present ground-breaking international plays to a London audience.

Today, the Gate exists to make international theatre that asks essential questions about ourselves, each other and the world. Our work investigates what it means to be alive now.

We imagine our work as a live conversation with our audience. Everyone is welcome. Our space transforms with every production – no two visits are ever the same.

We nurture the best and most diverse new talent to push the boundaries of what theatre is and what else it could be. We create space for radical, inventive thinking to surprise, delight, challenge and inspire.

Our mission and our approach to delivering it strives to embody our organisational values of community, diversity, invention, internationalism and sustainability.

gate@gatetheatre.co.uk
www.gatetheatre.co.uk

Follow @GateTheatre on Twitter and Instagram

To make a gift or join as a Gate Supporter
Please contact the Development Team on: development@gatetheatre.co.uk

The Gate Theatre is a registered charity (No. 280278).

The Gate Theatre Company is a company limited by guarantee.
Registered in England & Wales No. 1495543 | Charity No. 280278
Registered address: 11 Pembridge Road, Above the Prince Albert Pub,
London, W11 3HQ

Supported using public funding by
ARTS COUNCIL ENGLAND

ROSE
THEATRE

Rose Theatre is the largest producing theatre in South West London and has established itself since its 2008 opening as one of the most exciting theatres in the UK.

Recent Rose Original productions include: *Leopards* by Alys Metcalf, directed by Christopher Haydon and co-produced with *Fleabag* producer Francesca Moody Productions; *The Seven Pomegranate Seeds* by Colin Teevan, directed by Melly Still; Jeff James and James Yeatman's acclaimed adaptation of Jane Austen's *Persuasion* featuring an explosive foam party and a soundtrack of Frank Ocean, Dua Lipa and Cardi B; the critically acclaimed *Captain Corelli's Mandolin*, adapted by Rona Munro, which transferred to the West End in July 2019 following a successful UK tour; and the world premiere stage adaptation of Elena Ferrante's Neapolitan Novels, *My Brilliant Friend*, adapted by April De Angelis, which transferred to the National Theatre in November 2019. Both were directed by Rose Associate Artist Melly Still.

Forthcoming Rose Original productions include: Bertolt Brecht's masterpiece *The Caucasian Chalk Circle*, in a new version by Steve Waters with songs by Michael Henry and direction by Christopher Haydon, being developed in association with MGC; a brand-new retelling of Charles Dickens' timeless classic, *A Christmas Carol*, adapted by Morgan Lloyd Malcolm, featuring a female Scrooge and a wealth of local talent from the Rose Youth Theatre.

The Rose is home to one of the largest youth theatres in the country, offering over 1,200 participants training, careers advice and the opportunity to take part in productions alongside professionals.

rosetheatre.org

Kingston Theatre Trust, Company Limited by Guarantee. Registered in England and Wales.

Registered Charity 1000182.

Rose Theatre, 24-26 High Street, Kingston, KT1 1HL
+ 44 (0) 20 8174 0090

info@rosetheatre.org
rosetheatre.org

Follow @RoseTheatre on Twitter
Follow @rosetheatrekingston on Instagram
Like Rose Theatre at facebook.com/RoseTheatreKingston
Donate to Rose Theatre at rosetheatre.org/support-us/donate

For the Rose

A
SUDDEN
VIOLENT
BURST
OF
RAIN

Sami Ibrahim

Characters

ONE
  LANDOWNER'S SON
  WORKER
  LETTERS

TWO
  LANDOWNER
  GATEKEEPER
  LILY
  REGISTRAR'S REGISTRAR'S ASSISTANT
  WOMAN

THREE
  ELIF
  GRAN

Notes

The parts were written to be distributed between three actors, as shown above. But other combinations are possible.

Unattributed text should be divided up between the narrators.

A space tends to indicate a change of speaker – or at least a pause.

Narration is written in a regular font style – like this.

Dialogue is indicated in italics – *like this*.

The text should run through continuously but a star (*) is used to mark out shifts in the action – something like a new chapter.

There are very few stage directions but, in general, it would probably help if the staging isn't too literal.

This text went to press before the end of rehearsals and so may differ slightly from the play as performed.

It could start like this: ONE, TWO *and* THREE *sit around a portable paraffin stove.*

The flame is bright blue and licks at the battered saucepan above it.

Have you heard this story?

It starts with a woman
called Elif
sat on a stool in a field
holding clippers in one hand and a sheep in
the other.

Before long, that sheep was naked.
And cold.
Poor thing.
The woman patted it, it went on its way, the
next sheep arrived.
You can imagine the look on its face.
Just like that.
But the look on the woman's face: steely.
Buzz. Naked. Next.
Buzz. Naked. Next.
Muscles tensed and stretched, as she ripped
off thick parcels of wool.
This was work she did every day.
Up at four a.m: no exceptions.
And she didn't have any friends.
No hobbies, not much of a talker.
But she got on with it.
Every day: always working.

That day, she sat in a field near the coast.
Over there – just behind her – was a cart.
Her home.
As much as you could call it a home.

But it was where she slept, ate, did all the
things that happen behind closed doors.
And in front of her was the wide ocean.
Not that she noticed it.

And you might not think Elif's work was
important.
Shearing sheep.
But it was more than that.
You see, the wool accumulated as Elif sheared
it off.
Formed bundles.
And when enough wool had piled up – and
this is scientific fact.
Is it?
Oh yes: the density of that wool was so low
that it actually became buoyant.
The wool floated.
Rising into the sky.
It's how clouds are formed.
All the clouds in this corner of the island
came from her.
Every single one?
Thin ones, thick ones, woollen ones, real dark
bastard ones, sucking up moisture, collecting
rain and snow and hail and sleet.

And Elif needed to make sure these clouds
were fairly distributed.
Her time was spent travelling, sending up
clouds wherever they were needed.
Along the way, she had to herd the sheep.
Take care of them.
Feed them.
Clean up the dung, then pack up the cart,
travel all of the day, most of the night
sometimes, arrive at a new location, sleep,
wake up, ready to start again.

Except on this day, Elif paused.

She was tired.
And she knew she should be working but…
She felt the weight of her eyelids.
And she was trying to watch the sheep, make
sure they were okay as they…
But she couldn't help herself.
She muttered to herself…

ELIF   *Just for a moment. Just for a moment, I'll let
                my eyes…*

                *

Elif woke to discover blood.
A smear of it.
And then she saw
A trail of it.
And as she followed
A pool of it.
And then
A sheep.
Hi.
Not breathing.
Oh.
Thick red dripping from its neck.

It had wandered off.

ELIF   *Shit.*

Got caught in a wire fence.

This was sloppy work.
Made worse because the sheep weren't Elif's
sheep, were they?
They belonged to a Landowner.

Now, this Landowner owned everything in
this corner of the island.
Acres and acres of land.

Stretching far beyond the horizon.
And it was this land which Elif spent her days
travelling across, top to bottom, side to side.
The Landowner was Elif's boss, her
employer, and Elif felt indebted to her.
The Landowner also had a Son.
Elif felt attracted to him.
But that's for later.

Because this was the first animal to die under
Elif's watch.
She tried to stem the flow of blood but she
couldn't.
So Elif hauled the sheep up onto her back.
She decided to take it to the Landowner.

She knocked on a thick wooden door.
The Landowner
me
answered.
She saw Elif.
She saw the sheep.

LANDOWNER   *Come inside. Leave the animal.*

The sheep dropped to the ground with a thud.

In a wood-panelled drawing room, Elif sat in
front of her employer.
They were at a table: dark mahogany,
expensive.
A bit showy.
With a crackling fire.
Books lining the walls.
Bone china tea set.
The Landowner smiled, slid a cup over.

LANDOWNER   *A problem, was there?*

Elif decided it was best not to drink or speak.

LANDOWNER   *Looks like its neck got caught in wire.*

ELIF   –

LANDOWNER   *It happens. Are you to blame?*

ELIF   –

LANDOWNER   *Perhaps you weren't looking out for it*
              properly. I'd rather it didn't happen.

              The Landowner smiled again.

LANDOWNER   *Not that it can be helped.*
              An animal dies, an animal dies but

              Actually, can we pause it?
              Why?
              Because we're missing something.
              Because we know the Landowner is Elif's
              employer.
              But we don't know what kind of employee
              Elif is.
              She was a good employee, she worked hard,
              she didn't mess about.
              Which is fine but that wasn't the point.
              Because Elif wasn't born on this island.
              She had arrived here years earlier.
              Alone, no family.
              And, normally, when someone arrives on this
              island, they go to the far-off capital, they line
              up outside the King's palace, they register and
              they become a subject of our noble King.
              They are granted protection.
              But Elif
              scared and young
              and stupid
              had not done that.
              So when the Landowner said

LANDOWNER   *Do you know what happens to people who let*
              my animals die?

              With a smile.
              Elif was aware that the answer was not
              something she liked to think about.

She simply nodded and got up.
And the Landowner remained sat.
Watched as Elif walked out.
As she stormed out.
Past the Landowner's Son
who was stood right there

Oh. Me?

typically useless
as Elif opened the door.
Slammed the door.
Disappeared.

You see, there was something in the air back
then.
Still is.
Stories hanging on the wind.
Rumour was, one village over, a man had
disappeared, weeks back.
He'd got into a fight with another Worker.
A knife had slashed the man's skin.
The wound got infected, he couldn't work
properly.
Eventually he asked for medical help.
Instead, he was reported to the King and they
found out he wasn't a subject and suddenly
BAM
he was gone.
Stories like that raced through Elif's brain as
she tried to sleep.

The next morning, she woke earlier than
normal.
She worked harder than normal.
Sweated more.
Exhausted herself, her fingers became
scratched and bloody.
Then she packed up her belongings.
Herded the animals.
Was about to head off across the valley when

SON	*Excuse me?*
	a man approached through the mist
SON	*I'm sorry, I just wanted to*
	a man who seemed to float.
SON	*can you just hold on for a*
ELIF	–
SON	*Hi.*
ELIF	–
SON	*Not much of a talker are you?*
ELIF	*Only if it's necessary.*
SON	*Right. I get it.*
ELIF	–
SON	*I buried the animal – by the way – after you left.*
ELIF	*Thank you.*
SON	*Look: I'm sorry about my mother, my mum. She's under a lot of pressure, she's got her own problems, and she's difficult at the best of times so* *Are you okay?*
ELIF	*Yes.*
SON	*What are you staring at?*
ELIF	*I wasn't staring at you.*
SON	*What?*
ELIF	*No. I mean: I was staring at* *Nothing.* *I mean, not nothing, just*
SON	*I thought you weren't much of a talker?*
ELIF	*I'm not.*

SON	*Right.*
	I just wanted to say my mother, Mum, she's all bark.
ELIF	*Okay.*
SON	*In case you're worried.*
ELIF	*I'm not.*
SON	*Good.*
ELIF	*But I should be heading off.*
SON	*Do you need a hand or*
ELIF	*No.*
SON	*Cool. Yup. I, too, need to… do things.*

The Landowner's Son was not what you
would call 'formally employed'.
They never are.
But he was still a distraction.
Meaning Elif fancied the pants off of him.

SON	*Before you go, would you mind if I* *Maybe next time you travel near here, if I…*

And Elif tried not to get distracted by him.

ELIF	*I'd like that.*

But she didn't try very hard.
Because she fancied the pants off of him.
So he was hard to ignore.
Not when he had those gorgeous deep eyes.
And, Elif would think about him when she'd
leave, when she was away for
weeks
months
but he'd always be waiting

SON	*Hey.*
ELIF	*Hey.*

every single time.
Because he fancied the pants off of her.

And in between those snatched moments, he
turned up in Elif's dreams.
Usually naked.
And she tried not to look down, tried not to
stare at his, his
you know
his penis
but also she couldn't help staring at it and
obviously she liked what she saw, I mean she
really liked it, and at that point...
She got pregnant.

*

Which is typical.
What?
It starts with butterflies in your stomach.
A single butterfly.
Big one: churning and flapping.
Feels good.
No: it feels terrifying.
Night and day.
And Elif could barely concentrate because of
that fucking boy, with a smile she couldn't
say no to.

One day she kissed him.
He kissed her back.
Then he took out a necklace – beautiful
polished pearls – and placed it around her
neck.
Elif felt their cool indent on her skin, she
smiled at him.
And then she had to leave.
As she left, the butterfly flapped frantically.

She felt it endlessly.
As she worked.
As she travelled.
That butterfly would not stop flapping and so

She took a deep breath.
Calmed herself.
She reached down into her throat.
Right the way down.
Her fingers feeling their way through her body.
Into her tingling stomach.
She caught it.
This butterfly.
She lifted it out.
Held it in her clasped hand.
Saw its wings flapping.
Then slowing.
Then stopping.
The wings detached and fell to the ground
like autumn leaves.
The body remained in her hand.
It was a small seed.
She didn't know what to do with it.
She was stood near a river, she thought about
throwing it in.
But she couldn't bring herself to.
Instead, Elif took the seed over to her cart and
found a terracotta pot.
She filled it with soil, and then, with her little
finger, she hollowed out a small hole.
She placed the butterfly's body inside and
buried it.

*

Elif tended to the seed.
She watered it.

At one point, it grew so big she had to
transfer it to a bigger pot.
But she kept it with her, wherever she went.
She watched it grow – out the corner of her
eye – as she worked.

And every now and then, on her travels, she
saw the Landowner's Son.

SON   *Are you well?*

ELIF   *Good. Yes.*

SON   *Any news?*

ELIF   *Just that I've missed you.*

SON   *Me too.*

And some days, when they were together, Elif
would say next to nothing – she'd let the
hours drift by and he'd start to fill that silence
with sentences like

SON   *You know, I think I could spend a life with
         you.*

Sentences like

SON   *I think I could raise a family with you.*

And her response was not to smile or blush
it was to look around
at the small cart they were sat in
this place she called a home
with a terracotta pot in the corner
and ask him

ELIF   *What do you do when I'm not here?*

SON   *Nothing.*

ELIF   *Just by yourself, you do nothing?*

SON   *Yes.*

ELIF   *Twiddling your thumbs, absolutely nothing?*

SON	*I wait.*
ELIF	*Do you ever pity me?*
SON	*Why are you asking that?*
ELIF	–
SON	*Don't shrug, do you think I pity you?*
ELIF	*It's hard to tell.*
SON	*Of course I don't.*
ELIF	*You look at me funny sometimes.*
SON	*It's not looking at you funny, it's just* *Trying to figure you out.*
ELIF	*Figure what out? There's nothing to figure out.*
SON	*I barely know a thing about you.*
ELIF	*What do you want to know?*
SON	*Anything. Something.*
ELIF	*There isn't much.*
SON	*You could start by telling me what there is.*
ELIF	*I will.*
SON	*How about now?*

But then she'd need to leave.
Travel: north, west, east, south.
Herding the animals.
Packing up.
Gone.

All the while, that terracotta pot grew heavier.
Elif saw, beneath the soil, a child stirring.
Not yet ready to be unearthed but a head was
breaking the surface.
She had to find a bigger pot.
And then another.

And then
She didn't know.
Because this child was growing and
outgrowing the pot – shoulders pressed
against the clay.
And Elif saw wriggling.
She heard moaning.
Every night.
A crying.
As the cart trundled along muddy roads.
Every day.
As clouds flew up into the sky.
The child kept squirming and writhing and
expanding until there were no longer any pots
big enough for the child and at that point

Elif decided to stop.

She found a quiet corner, somewhere on the
edge of the Landowner's property.
Somewhere hidden, where the soil was damp
and rich.
And then
Carefully
Carefully
She lifted up the pot.
And she said

ELIF   *Here*.

Where you are right now.
She replanted her daughter in this soil.
Right here.
Where she decided her home would be.

And that felt good.
She thought.
That felt safe.

*

Of course, the Landowner wouldn't like it.
But Elif decided not to tell the Landowner.
Elif thought she could get away with it.
Hiding on a secret patch of land, refusing to travel.
She thought no one would notice.

But of course someone did notice.
The Landowner's Son.

Ugh.

SON	*What?*
ELIF	*It's good to see you.*
SON	*I thought you'd pass by a while back, I was waiting.*
ELIF	*I'm sorry. I got busy.*
SON	*With what?*
ELIF	*Just silly things.*
SON	*Okay.*
ELIF	*But I've missed you. A lot.*
SON	–
ELIF	*What is it?*
SON	*What's going on with you?*
ELIF	*Excuse me?*
SON	*It's just a question.*
ELIF	*I could ask you the same. I thought you're here to see me.*
SON	*I am.*
ELIF	*But…*
SON	*There's been floods.*

ELIF	*Where?*
SON	*This whole area. In the town, it's rained every day for the last three months, people were evacuated.*
ELIF	*I wasn't aware of that.*
SON	*Weren't you?*
ELIF	–
SON	*That fucking shrug.*
ELIF	*I don't know what you want me to say.*
SON	*How long have you been here?*
ELIF	*The normal amount of time.*
SON	*So all that extra rain has nothing to do with you?* *Nothing to do with you – I don't know – not travelling, not doing your job.*
ELIF	*I've been here for three months. I didn't think it would have an effect.*
SON	*Are you aware that we have no obligation to employ you?*
ELIF	*'We'?*
SON	*My mother and I. We pay you money, we give you shelter, all you have to do is complete the work.*
ELIF	*I'm doing my best.*
SON	*Don't make this more difficult than it is.*
ELIF	*I'm not, I'm just*
SON	*Look, we take on a risk when we hire you, we're doing you a favour, who else is going to give you work when you're, you're*
ELIF	*What?*

SON	*Do you have any idea the pressure we're under? If we want to make money we have to*
ELIF	*Pay me next to nothing.*
SON	*Yes.* *And there's plenty of others out there who'd take your pay.* *I'm sorry but it doesn't take much to find them.*
ELIF	–
SON	*I'm not trying to hurt you, I want to help.*
ELIF	*Oh thank you for clarifying.*
SON	*I'm giving you a second chance.*
ELIF	–
SON	*It's my job to do this, I don't enjoy it.*
ELIF	*Sure.*
SON	*But it would make things easier if you did your job too.*
ELIF	*Okay.*
SON	*Okay.* *Thank you.* *I was under the impression we meant something to each other.*
ELIF	*So was I.*
	–
SON	*Maybe I should be heading back.*
ELIF	*You know you've got a child on the way.*
SON	*What?*
ELIF	–
SON	*Why didn't you…?*

ELIF   –

SON   *What can I do to help?*

ELIF   *You can leave us.*

It rained as he dropped over the horizon.
It rained as Elif slept.
It rained as she woke.
It rained as
It rained a lot, that's all.
And as Elif sheltered from the rain, she sat in
her cart, she looked at all her belongings.
She looked at the sheep in the field.
She looked at her slowly sprouting child.
The slowly rotting wood of her home.
And she thought
Is this all I can offer?
To my child.
Is this the only life I can provide?
And she felt desperately alone.

*

The next morning, after her shift, Elif
travelled to the capital city.
Miserable journey: pissing with rain.
And she stood beneath the towering city
walls.
Looking up at the ramparts.

Through a peephole, a Gatekeeper eyed her.

GATEKEEPER *It's heavy rain that.*

ELIF   *Can you let me in?*

GATEKEEPER *What's your business?*

ELIF   *To see the King.*

GATEKEEPER	*The King himself? I doubt that. What's your purpose here, girl?*
ELIF	*To enquire about becoming a subject of the King.*
GATEKEEPER	*You'll be wanting the King's Registrar then.*
ELIF	*The who?*
GATEKEEPER	*Have you got an appointment?*
ELIF	*No.*
GATEKEEPER	*Of course not. They never think ahead.*
ELIF	*How do I get an appointment?*
GATEKEEPER	*By speaking to the King's Registrar's Registrar. Obviously.*
ELIF	*And how do I do that?*
GATEKEEPER	*You have to queue like everyone else.*
ELIF	*And where do I queue?*
GATEKEEPER	*Outside the King's palace.*
ELIF	*Good. Okay.*
GATEKEEPER	–
ELIF	*So are you going to let me in?*
GATEKEEPER	*If you ask me nicely.*
	–
ELIF	*Please.*
GATEKEEPER	*Any time! Good luck to you, girl, you'll need it.*
ELIF	*Arsehole.*

And the gates swung open.

She'd never been inside before.
She'd heard of it but had never imagined
anything like it.

All that glass and metal and stone and brick
scrambled up into the sky.
And then the traffic.
Noise.
Fumes.
Blocking her nose.
Black snot.
Drilling rain.
And the people.
Elif was rushed along in their current.
Like the whole population was being dragged
down a plughole.
Slipping past great dark structures.
Searing edifices.
Humans piled up on top of humans.
Stuffed into buildings whose architecture
yelled at you
GO AWAY
Until one building stood out.
A palace.
The only colourful building in the whole city.
It looked as if it were lined with jewels.
And statues – naked and perfect and white –
in various poses, with various beards and
muscles and fig leaves and breasts and fancy
hats all shining bright.
Elif looked up at it in wonder.
She thought how odd it was that this
magnificent building did the same job as her
small cart.
It was just walls and a roof.
For sleeping and eating and all the things that
happen behind closed doors.

Around the back of the palace was where the
people's business was conducted.
Near the drains.
Elif found a queue and stood in it.
A very long queue.

> Which took a very long time to shuffle forward.
> And when she did finally arrive at the front she asked for

ELIF   *The King's Registrar's Registrar? I need to make an appointment.*

> And the woman behind the glass pointed wearily
> to another queue.

ELIF   *I make an appointment over there?*

> And Elif went to stand at the back of this other, also-very-long queue, in which she waited to speak to the King's Registrar's Registrar's Assistant.
> Obviously.

> Next to her stood a man with a bright bruise under his right eye.

WORKER   *First day?*

ELIF   *Yes.*

WORKER   *Good luck.*

> An hour passed.

WORKER   *I come here most days, you know, nothing happens.*

> Then another hour.

WORKER   *They get funny about having you register anyway.*

ELIF   *Oh?*

WORKER   *They don't want you to work unless you're registered but they'll only register you if you can prove you can hold down a job but in order to register you can't actually have a job cos you have to stand outside here all day.*

ELIF	*What?*
WORKER	*Bunch of arseholes.*
	And another hour.
WORKER	*Anyway – you just here to register yourself?*
ELIF	*I want to make sure my daughter becomes a subject.*
WORKER	*Oh yeah. Classic. You slept with a native then?*
ELIF	*I'm sorry?*
WORKER	*Is he around too?*
ELIF	*Yes. No. Not exactly.*
WORKER	*Course not – took off, did he?*
ELIF	*I told him to do one.*
WORKER	*Good on you. As long as you've got proof I suppose.*
	Then two hours passed. And Elif couldn't concentrate and kept growing impatient until she
ELIF	*Sorry, what do you mean by 'proof'?*
WORKER	*As in proof that he's the dad.*
ELIF	*Right. Yeah. Sorry, why?*
WORKER	*So she can be registered.*
ELIF	*My daughter will be born on this island. She's entitled to the King's protection.*
WORKER	*Oh sweetie, you've got a lot to learn.*
	At which point a sign was put up in the King's Registrar's Registrar's Assistant's kiosk.
	CLOSED BACK TOMORROW NINE A.M.
	Bollocks.

*

It started with a sound.
This noise from a long way off: high-pitched
and sudden.
Then she felt a sharp stab in her stomach.
Then she saw the child's head popping out the
ground.
She was ready.
But also
she wasn't ready.
Blurry eyes.
Couldn't locate herself.
Like her brain was circling round her skull
growing dizzy
and nauseous
and then the
pain
as she reached the child
and then the
cries
as she saw her
emerging
the dirt and
the muck
trying to focus
brain like liquid
stepping
seeing
the child
the soil
screaming
like the soil was vibrating, this

aaaaaaaaaaaaaaaaaaaaaaaaaaaaaaaaaaaaaaaa

until it stopped.
As suddenly as it started.

Delicately
Elif brushed the soil away
and then
she lifted the child out.

She was beautiful.

Completely beautiful.

And a bit smelly.

Elif looked at the bottom of the hole and saw
a deposit of faeces.
In fact the child was overgrown.
She had roots hanging off her toes.
Those had to clipped.
And then she needed bathing.
But she was
absolutely, undoubtedly, undeniably

LILY   Me.
Mum called me Lily.
You know, like a flower: born of the soil.
It's a little obvious but the thought's nice,
isn't it?
Also she wanted a name that 'fitted in with
the natives'.
Hi.
I mean, I know it's rubbish, by the way.
Like, the story of butterflies in stomachs and
me growing out the earth, bulging out the soil,
it's
crap.
But Mum likes those kind of stories.
Livens life up, doesn't it?
Also, she gets funny when people say it like
it is.
You know: this bloke and my mum, they had
sex.
A lot.
It got her pregnant.

And then
Well. He dipped his wick and buggered off,
didn't he?
Ah. Sorry.
Spoiler alert: he was gone.
For good.

ELIF   *What?*

LANDOWNER   *He took off yesterday. With some woman.*

*

So Elif headed straight for the far-flung capital.
Determined, now.
She queued.
She filled out a form.
And handed in the form.
And was given another form.
Which she also filled out and handed back to
the King's Registrar's Registrar's Assistant,
who stamped it and smiled at Elif, who in turn
said

ELIF   *Is that it?*

and received the answer

KRRA   *We'll be in touch!*

ELIF   *Okay.*

KRRA   *Thank you!*

ELIF   *Um. What about my daughter?*

KRRA   *Your daughter can only be registered once
you're fully registered!*

ELIF   *Right. Will that take long, or…?*

KRRA   *As long as you're registered before she's
eighteen then she'll qualify automatically as
a subject of our great King!*

ELIF   *And, in your personal opinion, do you think*
                that's

KRRA   *Christ I don't know, love, I don't make the rules.*

                at which point Elif went home.
                And waited.
                Because that's what always happens.
                You wait.
                And as Elif waited, she smelt something...
                odd.
                She looked at Lily.
                She sighed.
                She changed Lily's nappy.
                Then fed her.
                Fed herself.
                Crawled into bed.
                Slept.
                Dreamt.
                Woke.
                Worked.
                And worked.
                She would strap Lily to her back and travel
                across the Landowner's territory.
                She would be away for days.
                Weeks sometimes.
                But she always came back.
                Here.
                Always.
                To check the letterbox at the edge of the field
                where Lily was born.
                Red.
                A little rusty.

LILY   The letterbox that is, not me.

                But it was empty.
                And Elif waited years.
                Literal years.

LILY   So long that I grew up.
                Birthdays flew by.
                Summers, winters.

But Elif never stopped.

LILY   I watched her never stop.
            Got annoyed at her never stopping.
            As nothing came.
            As I started asking questions.

            Awkward questions.

LILY   Reasonable questions.

            Questions that a child asks a parent, questions
            like

LILY   *What are you waiting for?*

ELIF   *Just a letter.*

            Questions like

LILY   *What's the letter?*

ELIF   *It's a letter that's going to take us far away
            from here.*

LILY   *Oh.*
            What's wrong with here?

            And then more questions, prying questions.

LILY   *Where's Dad?*

            Uncomfortable questions.

LILY   *Will he come back?*

            Impatient questions.

LILY   *What about your dad, where's he?*

            Or:

LILY   *What about your mum?*

ELIF   *She's…*

LILY   *She's what?*

ELIF   *At home. Where I was born. She'll visit us one
            day.*

LILY   *I'd like that.*

So now they waited for two things.
For a response from the King.
For a visit from Gran.

LILY   And neither came.

                Obviously.

LILY   Nothing.

                For a long time.

LILY   Nothing.

                As teeth burst through Lily's gums.

LILY   Nothing.

                As seasons flew by, as the earth spun round

LILY   Until something did turn up.
                Finally.
                A letter

                which told them

LETTER   *Hi, I'm a letter sent on behalf of the King.*
                I'm just letting you know that the King is
                willing to have you as his subject.
                But it may take a while.
                So you will have to wait.
                Also you'll have to take a test.
                Also you'll have to pay the King some money
                – these things aren't cheap you know!
                Yours sincerely,
                The King's Registrar's Registrar's Assistant's
                Underling.
                Thank you.

                –

                The letter didn't specify how much.
                Money, that is.
                But it didn't matter.
                Because this thing called money, it wasn't an
                issue.

*

That's a lie: money is always an issue.
Amen.

LILY   But me and Mum, we definitely didn't talk
              about money.
              It was not considered proper.

              When a school uniform had to be bought, it
              was bought.
              No questions.
              When books had to be bought

LILY   or new clothes

              Food

LILY   Birthday presents

              Christmas presents
              takeaway on a Friday night
              and now the washing machine's leaking
              and this thingamajig needs fixing, that
              whatchamacallit
              and then there's water
              electricity
              insurance for the
              whatever
              heating and petrol and new shoes

LILY   And all the things that kept Mum's bank
              balance treading water,
              it was all paid for.
              Just.

              Until another letter arrived, demanding:

LETTER   *An annual fee for processing your
              application.*

              And then another:

LETTER	*An overdue payment.*
	And another
LETTER	*A confirmation of NRPF.* *An appointment at the VCAS.* *A reminder to book your TOEIC, your* *QAVCIAPEONFHDBSNGBHJSKFGHS.*
ELIF	–
LILY	*Mum?*
ELIF	*Yes.*
LILY	*Is it going to be okay?*
ELIF	*Of course.*
LILY	–
ELIF	*Things aren't handed to you, Lily, you fight* *for them – do you understand?*
LILY	*I think so.*
ELIF	*My mother fought – properly – have I ever* *told you that?*
LILY	*No.*
ELIF	*She was a brave woman – made of iron –* *you've got that in your blood.* *You could peel back her skin and see the* *metal.* *She had to be.*
LILY	*Why?*
ELIF	*Her country – my country – was ruled by* *a tyrant.* *And the tyrant had all the power he wanted.* *He was clever about it too.* *He realised if other people had power then it* *meant he had less power.* *So he stole it all for himself.*

LILY   *No one stopped him?*

ELIF   *At a certain point, he had so much power, no*
              one could stop him.

LILY   *Except for Gran?*

ELIF   *No. Not even her.*

LILY   *Then what about Grandad?*

ELIF   *Your grandad was killed, Lily. In the middle*
              of the night.

LILY   *Why?*

ELIF   *Because he did a stupid thing.*
              He told people that the tyrant had to be
              stopped and people started to listen.
              But the tyrant had eyes and ears everywhere
              and the tyrant knew about your grandad.

LILY   *How was he killed?*

ELIF   *Very quickly. And Gran went to the police*
              station and she sat down and she looked
              the police officer right in the eye, she told him

              I wish to report a murder.

ELIF   *And the officer nodded, he made a note in his*
              little black book with his little pencil.

              It is the murder of my husband. It happened
              last night.

ELIF   *The officer kept taking notes, he asked for*
              details.
              What time of night, what Gran saw, what
              Gran heard, if Gran knew who did it.

LILY   *Did she?*

ELIF   *Your gran looked up: on the wall was*
              a picture of the tyrant.
              She looked at him, saw his dead eyes.

Then she pointed right at him.

He did. He murdered my husband.

LILY   *Did the tyrant go to jail?*

ELIF   *It was a long time ago.*
          The next day, Gran sent me here.

LILY   *Alone?*

ELIF   *Of course.*

LILY   *You mean you left her?*

ELIF   *I wasn't given a choice.*
          I was barely older than you.
          Gran gave away all her money to send me.
          She said, one day, she'd find a way to join me.

LILY   *But she didn't.*

ELIF   *She will. She'll arrive – in a boat – across the*
          sea. And we'll wave her into the harbour.
          We'll hug her. We'll take her by the hand and
          lead her to our home – an actual home that is
          ours – and eat a lavish meal and then sit, in
          silent content, sipping tea, knowing that no
          one can lay a finger on us.

LILY   I believed her when she told me that.
          I had that image in the my head: the ship in
          the harbour.
          Us waving it in.
          The low sunlight.
          I really did believe her.

          *

          On a normal morning, Elif was gone before
          Lily woke.
          On a normal morning, Elif was nowhere to
          be seen.

But on this particular morning
Elif was stood outside, waiting for Lily.
She wore a hat.
A nice hat.
And she was plastered with suncream.
Perfect.
Then she held out her hand and, grinning
deeply, said to her daughter

ELIF   *Fuck school. Fuck work.*

LILY   *Mum!*

ELIF   –

LILY   *Okay!*

And the two of them went off together.
Just them.
Like nothing else mattered.
Fuck it.
That day, there was a heatwave.
And then the next.
And the next.
No clouds.
On the radio, there was talk of a drought.
Talk of land being parched.
Choking from the heat, the blistering sun.

LILY   But me and Mum, we sat on a hill and ate ice
              cream.

              Vanilla for Elif.

LILY   Because she was boring and old.

              Double double caramel toffee fudge chocolate
              with sprinkles for Lily.

LILY   Because I was cool and young.

              And the sun beat down across endless days
              as they watched the sheep grazing in the fields
              below.

–

LILY	*What are we doing here?*
ELIF	*You'll see.*
LILY	*What about work, don't you have to*
ELIF	*I said you'll see.*

–

So they waited.
They watched the sheep.
Who had gone too long without a good
shearing.
And who now
started to puff up.
Like balloons.
No: like pastry in the oven.
Covered in this thick wool
which kept swelling
and
as true as true can be
one of them started to float.

The two of them watched it.
It let out this strange sort of

aargh!

as its feet disconnected from the ground.
And then another did the same.
And another.
Now they were like balloons.
Floating in the air.
A whole parade of flying sheep, each one
blotting out the sun, covered in this wild
mane of thick wool.
And they bounced along the prevailing winds.
And Elif stood.
She turned to Lily.

ELIF	*Come on then.*

And they both tottered along, behind the
sheep, gazing up at the sky.

LILY   It was one of the few happy days we spent
together.
Lodged in my memory.

As they followed the sheep drifting towards
the far-off capital.
As these sheep glided over the walls of the
city.
As a few grey subjects looked up.
A little confused, at first, because clouds don't
normally go

baaaa!

but then the people realised what was
happening.
They started to stare
and point
and shout
at these sheep
who were only animals, remember, with
animal instincts, and they

Well: nature called.
And the sheep proceeded to cover the whole
city in shit.

It was glorious.
Seeing the subjects of our great capital
splattered in excrement.
All the people who sent complicated letters to
Elif.
Who demanded money.
Who patronised her.
Who sneered at her.
Who told her

You're welcome to go home any time you like!

Here they were: ducking for cover, wading
through the slop.
Like expert drone strikes: discharge from
above: precision-targeted, faecal chaos.

LILY   But as we traipsed back home, I couldn't
              figure Mum out.
              She was silent.

              She was scared.

              She was confident.

LILY   She was steeling herself for

              the Landowner.

              *

              Who was waiting for mother and daughter
              and whose face
              was the brightest of reds.

              Lily listened from outside.
              She expected loud noises and shouting but
              Instead
              Inside
              Elif simply handed over a letter.
              From the King's Registrar's Registrar's
              Assistant's Underling.

LANDOWNER   *How are you affording all this?*

ELIF   *I'm not.*

LANDOWNER   –

ELIF   *But, until you help, I will not work.*

LANDOWNER   *I see.*

ELIF   *Well?*

LANDOWNER *There are plenty more where you came from.*

ELIF *Except you won't find anyone who doesn't need training.*

LANDOWNER *I'm not sure about that.*

ELIF *You know, you should be scared of me.*
I have been hired illegally.
I can report you as much as you can report me.

LANDOWNER *But I don't think you will. And I would suggest that means we need each other.*

ELIF *I'll work if you help me.*
I'll work like before – harder than before.
I have to make this year's payment and then, then

LANDOWNER *Okay. Can I sit?*

ELIF *–*

LANDOWNER *The child outside, what's her name?*

ELIF *Lily.*

LANDOWNER *This money, you believe it will provide a future for Lily?*

ELIF *It will cement it.*

LANDOWNER *Good. Then I want to be a part of that future.*

ELIF *What?*

LANDOWNER *If I am spending more of my money I want to be certain you do a correct job of raising that child.*

ELIF *–*

LANDOWNER *If you want to live on this island, Elif, you have to put up with the rain.*

ELIF *No.*

LANDOWNER	*Think before you answer.*
ELIF	*She's mine, no one raises her but me.*
LANDOWNER	*I'm offering you the money.*
ELIF	*And I deserve it with no strings attached –* *I work hard enough.*
LANDOWNER	*You do.* *But if I give you that much money then I start* *to lose money.*
ELIF	*Lose money?*
LANDOWNER	*Like when I have to replace dead sheep.*
ELIF	*–*
LANDOWNER	*Times are tougher than you think, I'm being* *generous. And I've let that child live here for* *a while, so now I'm asking for something in* *return for that generosity.*
ELIF	*I'm not sure.*
LANDOWNER	*What happens if you're successful? If the* *King grants you his protection?*
ELIF	*I keep working for you, I stay loyal, I'm clear* *on that.*
LANDOWNER	*It doesn't sound clear.* *Sounds like it might get sticky – doesn't it?* *Like then you can turn around and leave,* *I never see you again.*
ELIF	*You can trust me.*
LANDOWNER	*Says the person with nothing to lose.*
ELIF	*Please.*
LANDOWNER	*Oh come on. Please. I am not negotiating via* *pity.*
ELIF	*I don't want your pity.*

LANDOWNER   *You could've fooled me.*
             Perhaps we're done here.

ELIF   *She's your grandchild. Outside. She is your*
             Son's child.

LANDOWNER   *I know.*

ELIF   *So you'll know he was selfish to leave her.*

LANDOWNER   *I thought you asked him to leave.*
             Or have I misremembered?

ELIF   *The point is that I want what's best for her.*

LANDOWNER   *Which is what I want too.*

ELIF   *I don't believe that.*

LANDOWNER   *I do.*

ELIF   –

LANDOWNER   *And technically, she is my family as well.*

ELIF   *She has nothing to do with you.*

LANDOWNER   *Fine.*
             How old is she now?

ELIF   *Thirteen.*

LANDOWNER   *And is she a good kid?*

ELIF   *Yes. Very.*

LANDOWNER   *A fighter?*

ELIF   *Like her mum.*

LANDOWNER   *Good.*
             If you don't accept, I want you both gone by
             morning.

*

LILY	We left immediately.
	We took sleeping bags.
	A little food.
	Water.
	Left everything else.
	The thing is, Mum says I'm a fighter.
	I'm not.
	I know I wasn't
	As we huddled outside the walls of the capital.
	As the gate was locked and all sorts of lonely figures turned up.
	Some stared, some wandered on.
	They looked exhausted.
	Mum held me close as I shivered.
ELIF	*We're going to be okay.*
LILY	She said that more than once.
ELIF	*We are, in this country we can be.*
LILY	*Why didn't we stay?*
ELIF	*Because we weren't welcome.*
LILY	*But it's cold out here.*
ELIF	*So we'll find a place where it's warm.*
LILY	*Where?*
ELIF	*I don't know, we'll find it in there.*
LILY	*We should have stayed.*
ELIF	*That would have been a bad idea.*
LILY	*She was trying to help us.*
ELIF	*She was not helping us.*
LILY	–
ELIF	*There's work in the city, okay? In there, people are hired to hoover up the rain.*

LILY   *So what?*

ELIF   *So it's good work*
            And this is a good thing: we'll have our own
            lives to lead.

LILY   *Okay.*

ELIF   *Do you believe me?*

            –

LILY   Mum arrived in this country illegally, she
            stayed here illegally, started searching for
            a home and then got us kicked out of the
            closest thing we ever had to a home.
            She made up stories about it.
            Then told me those stories.
            Comforting stories.
            Scary stories.
            Whatever stories.
            Stories that she thought would help.
            And they do help.
            They did: sometimes.
            But there comes a point where the stories stop
            helping.

            –

ELIF   *Do you believe me?*

LILY   And after one night sleeping outside, we
            needed
            Shelter.
            Anything.

ELIF   –

LILY   Mum went off
            inside the capital walls
            and I waited in the cold.
            Until she came back for me.

                    *

The necklace, the one the Landowner's Son
had bought her, Elif sold it.
She used the money to pay for her and Lily to
have accommodation
if you can call it accommodation
but it was a room, all to themselves
in a house shared by
ten, fifteen?
People came and went but they were all
squashed
miserable
in this two-up, two-down.
And the room itself – Elif and Lily's room –
couldn't have been bigger than
this space.
Roughly.
With a single bed.
And a mattress on the floor.
Sink in the corner.
Portable paraffin stove.
Wardrobe.

LILY   Torn carpet.
Moths.
It was a shithole.
And it could've been worse.
But now we lived in the capital it meant
Well.
Rent.
Food.
Travel.
Everything
was expensive.
And small.
You paid more, you got less – that was the rule.

Elif found the work she wanted from a
neighbour.
'Neighbour' meaning the man who slept in
the next room.

He was a Worker.
Bright bruise under his right eye.
On Elif's first day, he took her to the edge of
the capital.
They followed a tributary along the city walls.

WORKER   *The pay's shit but it's all cash-in-hand so no
one asks any questions.*

ELIF   *This is where you dump the water.
It all flows downstream and then someone
else deals with it.*

           –

WORKER   *Do you have any questions?*

ELIF   *I thought no one asked any.*

WORKER   *Very good.*

ELIF   *If we don't clear away the rain, the city fills
up like a bowl of soup.*

WORKER   *So just avoid that and you'll be alright.
If you're lucky, there's a heatwave: means we
don't have to come in.*

ELIF   *It also means some poor arsehole's been
deported.*

WORKER   *So it's swings and roundabouts – you keeping
up?*

ELIF   *Yup.*

WORKER   *One time, we had a heatwave and I thought
Lucky me!
but there was actual animal shit everywhere –
like it had literally fallen from the sky!
Worst week of my fucking life. And that stink.
Jesus wept – don't get anything clogged in
there, you hear me?*

ELIF   *Because the hoovers can't handle anything
other than water.*

WORKER   *And another thing*

LILY   And Mum said he went on for a while.
        But he had kind eyes.
        Apparently.

        Sometimes he and Elif took the train together
        in the mornings.
        It was nice.
        Then his work rota would shift and Elif
        wouldn't see him for months.
        No big deal, it happens.
        But then his rota would shift back.
        And they'd pick up again.
        Neither took it too seriously.
        Except for some nights – when the two
        bumped into each other.
        And other nights, when Elif found the Worker
        waiting for her, just outside the door.
        On those nights, Lily was told to wait on the
        landing.

LILY   I hated that.
        Of course I did.
        It didn't help that I moved schools.
        And hated that too.

        She had a friend though.
        Sometimes she hung around at that friend's
        house.
        It was fine.
        It was better than the room she lived in.

        Then, one time, she overheard her friend's
        mum whispering

        Why does she smell?

LILY   *What?*

        And the next day, the friend asked

        Can we go back to yours?

LILY   *No. Obviously not.*

                        They stopped being friends after that.
                        Lily spent a lot of time, alone, in the small
                        room with faded walls.

                        She remembers watching TV.
                        She remembers images on the TV of men,
                        mostly men, in small boats, trying to scramble
                        onto the shore.
                        She remembers feeling proud that she was
                        already on this shore.
                        She remembers feeling angry.
                        She remembers wondering if it was all worth
                        the risk, then switching off the TV and trying
                        to sleep.

LILY   Mum was out most hours anyway.

                        Usually working.

LILY   Or spending time with the slimy man.

                        Or queueing up outside the King's palace.
                        Because more letters were arriving.

LILY   Endless letters.

                        Letters demanding

LETTER   *That you register weekly!*

                        Or:

LETTER   *That you take this extra test!*

                        Or:

LETTER   *That you pay this extra*

LILY   Can you fuck off.

LETTER   –

                        and at night, Lily drifted off to sleep in an
                        empty room.
                        She had empty dreams.
                        Then empty days.

LILY   And some afternoons I'd come home from
                school and he'd just be there.
                That slimy man.
                His bright bruise.
                First he'd wait outside the door.
                Then he'd be in our room.
                In our room.
                Like it was his.
                And mostly you ignore shit like that.
                Open door – see slimy man – leave.
                But when it happens again and again.

WORKER   *Alright?*

LILY   You start to think enough's enough.

                *

WORKER   *Don't mind me.*

LILY   *What are you doing in here?*

WORKER   *Your mother said I should pop round.*

LILY   *She's not here though, is she?*

WORKER   *Doesn't look like it.*

LILY   *So can you get out?*

WORKER   *I'm waiting to talk to her.*

LILY   *You can wait outside.*

WORKER   *If she wanted me to wait outside, she wouldn't
                have given me a key.*

LILY   –

WORKER   *I'll keep myself to myself.*

LILY   *So what, you like her then?*

WORKER   *I'm sure that's not your business.*

LILY   *Do you though?*

WORKER   *We take things slow.*

LILY   *But do you actually like her or do you just*
              hate living in a room with four other men?

WORKER   *Bit of both.*

LILY   *Does she know that?*

WORKER   *I'm sure she does.*
              I'm not the only one who tried it on with her,
              I'm just the only one she said yes to.

LILY   –

WORKER   *I'm not trying to cause trouble, you know,*
              I just like being with her.

LILY   *If you ever think of*

WORKER   *hurting her? I'm not doing that.*
              Christ, she'll do it to herself, she keeps
              working the way she does.

LILY   *She's doing fine.*

WORKER   *How do you know, do you see much of her?*

LILY   *A little.*

WORKER   *I mean, I barely see her so I don't see how*
              you would.

LILY   *She's just busy.*

WORKER   *You're telling me.*

              –

LILY   *Is that why you're here then?*

WORKER   *What?*

LILY   *I dunno, figure out if she's too busy for you?*

WORKER   *Not far off.*

LILY   *Is the sad little grown man feeling a bit*
              starved of attention? Poor thing.

WORKER   *I'm thinking of leaving.*

LILY   *Oh. What, like the city?*

WORKER   *Like this island.*
              Like forever.
              I just want to know if it's worth hanging
              around for your mum.

LILY   *Hanging around? She won't go with you.*

WORKER   *Of course she won't.*
              But she might have an opinion about whether
              I leave.

LILY   *She told me you were trying to register.*

WORKER   *I was.*

LILY   *So?*

WORKER   *I'm tired. It's expensive. It won't make a*
              difference.

LILY   *Course it makes a difference.*

WORKER   *Oh yeah, that piece of paper saying:*
              'Welcome to our little island, we no longer
              want you to piss off.'
              And that changes everything, does it?

LILY   *Yes.*

WORKER   *How? Where?*

LILY   *It just does.*

WORKER   *What, in your gut? Or your heart? What*
              difference does it make to a human?

LILY   –

WORKER   *People give it all that, you know, oh yeah, we*
              all live under the same sky.

	It's just that, beneath that sky, there's some arsehole saying 'don't stand here, stand over there and shut your mouth'.
LILY	*You actually think that?*
WORKER	*You'll understand when you're older.*
LILY	*I don't think I will cos I'm not growing up to be a quitter.*
WORKER	*I'd call it common sense, not quitting.*
LILY	*Of course you would.*
WORKER	*It's not something a fourteen-year-old can get their head around.*
LILY	*Fifteen.*
WORKER	*Oh. Your mother said fourteen.*
LILY	–
WORKER	*You know what, it's late.* *Tell her I said goodbye.*
LILY	He left the key by the sink. And it was my turn to wait for Mum.
ELIF	*We'll talk later.*
LILY	The same excuse. Always
ELIF	*Later.*
LILY	Always
ELIF	*In a minute.*
LILY	Always
ELIF	*Lily, please.*
LILY	And she missed him, by the way, you could tell.
ELIF	*Of course I don't miss him.*

LILY   But she did.

ELIF   *I don't need anyone but you.*

LILY   But that wasn't true, it obviously wasn't true.
              Because every time she said

ELIF   *We're fine as we are.*

LILY   It felt
              I don't know.
              And her skin became
              like when you butcher an animal, hang it up,
              drain its blood.

ELIF   *Oh stop it.*

LILY   *You need sleep.*

ELIF   *I'm fine.*

LILY   And then she was off. Again. And the small,
              faded room felt cavernous.

                      *

              One morning Lily woke up and decided to
              give her friend a bruise

LILY   under her left eye.
              Cos I spent a few weeks *not* going to school
              and when I turned up, she slagged Mum off
              so I decided she was better off
              splat
              on the floor.
              I thought it suited her.
              But Mum got called in
              missed a shift
              and when everyone
              and I mean everyone
              had finished bollocking me
              we went back to the room and we

ELIF	–
LILY	We sat in silence.
ELIF	–
LILY	You know, for quite a while.
	–
ELIF	*If I miss more than half a shift I don't get paid for any of it.*
LILY	*Oh. I'm sorry.*
ELIF	*It's gone now so*
LILY	–
ELIF	*Are you going to explain it or just sit there?*
LILY	*I, um, I don't know.*
ELIF	*You don't know why you hit someone? You need a better reason than that.*
LILY	*Sorry.*
ELIF	*I'm still not hearing a reason.*
LILY	*I don't know.* *I haven't seen you in a while, I guess.*
ELIF	*Okay.*
LILY	*Not that that's got anything to do with* *I mean it sort of*
ELIF	*You wanted my attention, is that it?*
LILY	*Maybe.*
ELIF	*So here I am.*
LILY	–
ELIF	*What is it? Say what you want to say.*
LILY	*Fuck, Mum, there's not a thing I can just say, it's*

ELIF	*What?*
LILY	*Nothing.*
ELIF	*You think I work too much.*
LILY	*A bit. Maybe.*
ELIF	*What does maybe mean?*
LILY	–
ELIF	*Don't shrug, lift up your chin, tell me.*
LILY	–
ELIF	*I'm doing my best for you.*
LILY	*I know.*
ELIF	–
LILY	*I know and I love you for it.*

Hang on.

LILY	*I know and I love you so much for it.*

Is this

LILY	*I love you so much for everything you've scarified, for everything you*

Is this what you really said?

LILY	–

Is it?

LILY	–

Lily turned to her mother.

ELIF	*I'm doing my best.*

And she said

LILY	*Well maybe your best is not very impressive.*

And Elif said

ELIF	*I sacrifice a lot for you.*

And Lily said

LILY   *What, by sleeping with random men?*

ELIF   –

LILY   *And then ignoring me, acting like you don't have a daughter?*

ELIF   *That's not*

LILY   *I am telling you what it is like, growing up without you here.*

ELIF   *I am always here.*

LILY   *What, in spirit? In your thoughts? And when you do turn up, you're not even a person, you're a husk, you're a ghost.*

ELIF   *Do you understand why I work?*

LILY   *Yes.*

ELIF   *Do you understand the situation we're in, that there is nowhere else to go?*

LILY   *Yes.*

ELIF   *So I think this conversation is over.*

LILY   *It's just you care about him more than you care about me.*

ELIF   *What? You don't believe that.*

LILY   –

ELIF   *Lily.*

LILY   *I always wanted to speak the language you grew up with, did you know that?*
        Like Gran.
        But you never taught me, never had the time, never even told me about my own family, about what it was like back home, like it doesn't exist.

ELIF	*Your home is here.*
LILY	*Is it? A boxroom in a run-down house in a shit part of a city in a country that you've spent years trying to prove is our home – but has never wanted us.*
ELIF	*I don't teach you another language because it is harder to deport someone if they don't speak the language of the country they're being sent to.* *You understand?* *Because if you turn eighteen and I'm still not registered.* *Forget it.* *I want this island to be your home because it is better and you deserve better.*
LILY	*Maybe I don't want this place to be my home.*
ELIF	*Don't be stupid.*
LILY	*Maybe I don't like the weather. Or the people, or the rules, or the dirt, the smog, this city, the things you have to do to survive in this city, the things you learn, the fact that, on every bit of cash, there is a picture of the person who decides whether we get to stay, like they're watching us, constantly, going 'don't fuck it up' and then there's the food. And the milk always goes off. And this room. And the people, did I mention the people?*
ELIF	*You did.*
LILY	*I don't like it when they spit on me.*
ELIF	*Is that all they do?*
LILY	–
ELIF	*I don't like it either. But I accept it.*
LILY	Then I um

I told her to suck my arse.
Not big, not clever.
But I was a teenager so
That put a proper end to the conversation.

*

But, you know, the next day Elif went into her
work and said to her boss

ELIF   *Can I change my shift?*

And he agreed.
And Elif spent time with Lily.

LILY   A weekend.
An actual weekend.

They went to a park.
They ate ice cream.
They sheltered from the rain under a tree.
And then another letter came.
Obviously.

LETTER   *Another extension fee!*

And another and suddenly

ELIF   *Can I switch again?*

Suddenly

ELIF   *Can I take on another shift?*

LILY   And we were back to normal.
Cos nothing changes.

And when she asked for more shifts, Elif got
moved to the posh side of town.
Hard work lugging the vacuum cleaner across
the city.
Same hours, more travel.
She stood outside towering houses.

Emptying the streets.
And the rain wouldn't stop.
It fell down in bucketloads.
Each thick drop plummeted onto her back.
The machine barely coped.
The nozzle kept vomiting up this
grey
sludge-like
liquid.
And Elif struggled with it alone.
The Worker was gone.
Lily was at school.
And the water kept rising.
And rising.
And the machine kept spluttering.
And choking.
Until she bashed it.
Hard.
And out of the nozzle came a necklace.

As if from nowhere.
From above.
Beautiful necklace: white pearls.
Someone must have dropped it.

It must have been clogging up the machine.

Elif stared at it.

No one else was around.
She made sure of that.

Then she put it in her pocket.

She kept it in her pocket.

She didn't know why.
She didn't want to keep it.
She didn't want to give it away.
It reminded her of the necklace the
Landowner's Son had given her.
The pearls looked so...

	And she thought to herself
ELIF	*I haven't stolen it. I've borrowed it.*
	Then she went home. She watched Lily sleeping. Always on the mattress. Never on the bed.
	And the next day, Elif went back to the same neighbourhood. More rain. And she kept the necklace in her pocket. And as she revved up the machine, she heard a
WOMAN	*Excuse me? Excuse me?!*
ELIF	–
WOMAN	*Sorry. You were here yesterday, yes? I saw you from my window.*
ELIF	–
WOMAN	*You speak English?*
ELIF	*No.*
WOMAN	*Oh. Um. YOU WERE HERE YESTERDAY? HERE? YESTERDAY? CLEANING?*
ELIF	–
WOMAN	*Yes? Is that a yes?*
ELIF	–
WOMAN	*DID YOU FIND A NECKLACE? ON THE FLOOR?*
ELIF	–
WOMAN	*I DROPPED MY NECKLACE. DID YOU FIND IT?*
ELIF	*No.*

And Elif fired up the vacuum cleaner.
Sucked up the rainwater.
Except the woman didn't leave.

WOMAN   *EXCUSE ME?*

She hung around.
She stopped a passer-by.
She pointed.
She waited.
She kept waiting.
Under an umbrella.
Checking her watch.
Checking her phone.
And every now and then

WOMAN   *EXCUSE ME?*

Above the roar of Elif's machine.

WOMAN   *EXCUSE ME?*

Until Elif walked over and

WOMAN   *Oh are you going to speak to me now?*

ELIF   *I don't have your fucking necklace.*

More rain.
And the machine started to break.
Water around the ankles.
And then a man turned up.
The husband.
Black suit, grey skin.
Who spoke to the woman.
Then walked over
asked if Elif would stop
asked if

ELIF   *What do you want?*

SON   *Elif?*

ELIF   *Shit.*

SON   *What are you…?*

ELIF   –

SON   *Elif, it's me.*

ELIF   *I know.*

SON   *It's been so long, it must've been*

ELIF   *You live in one of these houses?*

SON   *Yes.*

ELIF   –

SON   *How are you?*

ELIF   –

SON   *I asked my mother, Mum where you'd ended up but she never said.*

ELIF   *Because we left.*

SON   *I know.*

ELIF   *After you left.*

SON   *You told me to leave.*

         –

ELIF   *Is that her then?*

SON   *Yeah.*

ELIF   *You're happy?*

SON   *We're alright.*

ELIF   *Good.*

SON   *But*
         um
         for some stupid reason she thinks you've stolen her necklace.

ELIF   *I have.*

SON   *Oh. Right.*

ELIF	*I found it, I liked it, it's probably worth a lot of money.*
SON	*A little, yeah.* *But it's, um, you know, it's different from the one I gave you.*
ELIF	*Not that different.*
SON	*Did you keep it?*
ELIF	*I sold it. I had to find accommodation for me and my daughter.*
SON	*Of course. How is your daughter?*
ELIF	*She's yours too.*
SON	*I know.*
ELIF	*Does she know?*
SON	–
ELIF	*Lily's doing well. Better than you can imagine.*
SON	*Lily. Good.*
ELIF	*So what, you gonna call the police or something?*
SON	*No.*
ELIF	*Cos I'm not giving it back.*
SON	*Keep it.*
ELIF	*Why?*
SON	*Sell it, make money, hold on to it, I don't care.*
ELIF	*Your wife's standing right there.*
SON	*I'll make something up.*
ELIF	–
SON	*Take it. I want to help.*

ELIF   *Don't say that.*

SON   *It's not charity, I just*

ELIF   *Want to feel less guilty.*

                The water was rising.
                At that moment it was around their calves.

SON   *Turn around and leave.*

                It was clinging to their legs.

SON   *Go.*

                And Elif turned.
                She left.
                And as Elif left
                The woman was shouting
                As Elif left
                The husband told her

SON   *Leave it.*

                But the woman wouldn't.
                Of course she wouldn't.
                And Elif stumbled as the waters grew.
                And as the waters grew
                the woman shouted

WOMAN   *Fucking stop her.*

                As the waters grew
                a wave crashed through the city.

                It was a flood that consumed everything.

                And Elif walked home to Lily.

                Calmly.

                Through the cascading waves.

                Breathing steadily.

                Feeling the water bounce off her skin.

                                    *

LILY	*Mum?*
ELIF	*Get up.*
LILY	*What's going on?*
ELIF	*Get up, we're going.*
LILY	*Why?*
ELIF	*Because I said so. Pack your things.*
LILY	And she dragged me out of bed, no explanation, just
ELIF	*We're going now.*
LILY	Quick walk to the bus station. Where she knelt, gripped my shoulders, looked me in the eye.
ELIF	*You have to stay calm.*
LILY	*What is it?*
ELIF	*It's nothing.*
LILY	Until
ELIF	*It's nothing.*
LILY	Until, we saw, through the station door
ELIF	*Nothing.*
LILY	We saw them coming, we
ELIF	*We saw nothing.*
LILY	*Mum?*
ELIF	We disappear in the middle of the night and no one stops us. First thing I did was sell the necklace for less than it was worth and more than I could ever imagine, then we got on a bus, left the city, ate crisps as the landscape sped by, got off again, waited for another bus, and arrived before dawn at the spot where Lily was born

and the field was as it had always been, apart
from someone else, whoever-it-was, who had
moved in and was living in a static caravan
balanced on cinder blocks, right at the edge of
the field, and before whoever-it-was could
wake up, we found some wire round the back
of the caravan, we found some posts, we built
a fence around the field, finished it in the hour
and looked at our work ever so proudly, and
people complained, whoever-it-was
complained, but it didn't matter – it was our
field – we made it ours, we had money, we
were immovable and the first thing we did
was set up a border, tight controls, we found
bricks and we cemented the fence, made it
impenetrable so by the time the police turned
up, we were ready to declare independence:
we had a set of ideals, we had a constitution,
we declared ourselves the first and only
citizens of a new country, a new home, and
then we built a palace – for us, covered in
glorious naked statues – and we had an
election – which I won – and afterwards, a
delegate from the British government was
sent, the same British government that was in
chaos, dealing with floods and famine, but
I refused to speak to the delegate, kept him
waiting for a long time, out by the drains, just
to prove a point, after which we had support
rolling in, the Kurds backed us, Taiwan, the
people of Palestine, Ukraine tipped its hat,
Kosovo, Catalonia jumped on board, not
exactly big dogs but we went to the UN and,
despite opposition, they recognised us as a
sovereign nation, gave us a seat at the table,
all the while, to the south of the field, we
started mining, deep in the earth we found
reserves of copper, tin, lithium, silver, gold,
which we used to establish a formal currency,

began trading, made a healthy profit and, sure,
a few trees died, the ground curdled, but we
began negotiations on the international stage,
we set up a central bank, borrowed against
our reserves, established a housing market,
you could get a decent house and garden for
a decent price, there was a financial market,
a strong banking sector, and of course – in the
north of the field – we had the sheep, which
Lily took care of, overseeing agriculture,
a stable food supply, sending clouds over to
our international neighbours, which sounds
generous you might think, but it also meant
we controlled resources, we controlled the
weather, we wrestled it into submission and
when our neighbours got angry, threatened to
invade, we stopped shearing, let them have a
heatwave, starved them, and once we realised
how vulnerable they were, we strangled those
resources, we invaded them because we
needed access to the sea, so we pushed west,
down to the shore, found a natural harbour,
felt sand between my toes and when I realised
just how easy it was, this invasion business –
well – we bought weapons of war on the
international market, imported them on huge
iron ships, hired mercenaries, ranks of troops,
paid for training, intelligence, launched an
assault, let our borders expand, we
steamrolled across the British Isles, we
captured territory and watched on as our
nation unfurled, as we set up a capital in
Exeter, then Bristol, Reading, charging up the
M4 and as we went east, refugees flooded
west and we welcomed them, raised the gates,
we gave them land and work, food and a
temperate climate, and we recognised every
single one of them – me personally – I did –
I would look each one of them in the eye as

they entered through our great city gates,
I would think, we were fighting for
something, for them, as we gave them a
proper education, as we gave them a strong
welfare net, healthcare, social care, security,
funding for the arts, increased international
aid, and, yes, we made sacrifices, we accepted
economic sanctions when they came, we had
to enforce military service and a great many
died – in war, down the mines, starvation –
but we honoured them, in moments of silence,
with symbols and monuments and buildings
as we sung of patriotic glories, as we drank
and ate and threw up and watched fireworks
and saluted and listened to speeches and then
wrote books, great tomes detailing the
privilege of great sacrifice, of tilting to the
future, of seeing off threat after threat after
threat, of not stopping for a second as we
scramble over our enemies as we maintain
and protect what we have built, this land that
bonds us like metal, fused together, eternal
and firm, a cold iron path stretching into the
past, into the future, unbreakable and safe,
a simple home, here.

*

LILY *and* ONE *sit around the portable paraffin stove – the
saucepan is now boiling, steam rising.*

THREE *watches on, not quite visible.*

LILY   *She was arrested.*
                 *Something to do with a necklace that she'd
                 stolen or*
                 *I don't know, it's such a blur, it all happened
                 at the bus station.*

And I don't know where she was trying to take
me but
Anyway, after the arrest, they realised who
she was, her status, she was transferred
to a detention centre.
Outskirts of the city, busy A-road, threatening
to deport her, you know, the usual.

ONE   *I'm sorry.*

LILY   *Nah. It's alright.*

ONE   *What's happening to her now?*

LILY   *I don't know.*
            They dragged her off me and led her away.
            They were very polite – the officers – they
            smiled a lot.
            That was the last time I saw her.

ONE   *You don't get in touch?*

LILY   *I tried. Those places are like black holes, and*
            she's just stuck.
            She could be dead for all I know.

ONE   *Don't think like that.*

LILY   *Who knows? It's just another story, everyone's*
            got one.

ONE   *So?*

LILY   *It got me here anyway.*
            You know: fuck social services, I'll make my
            own way thank you very much.
            Still had that room, stayed there for a bit, did
            shifts at Mum's old work.
            Hated it.
            Quit.
            Sold off anything I could.
            Came down here, I wasn't born far actually.
            But then I needed money and I've gotta
            support myself so…

ONE   *Do you miss her?*

LILY   –

ONE   *You'll hear from her eventually. There'll be*
             court proceedings, you'll go back
             home, you'll find other work. Anyway, you'll
             be alright, you're only seventeen.

LILY   *Actually, it's my birthday today.*

ONE   *Oh. I'm sure she's thinking of you.*

LILY   –

             *

THREE   Lily turns eighteen and, on a computer,
             somewhere in a big grey building, in a big
             grey city, a file updates.

LILY   What?

ONE   And... one thing simply shifts to another.

THREE   But Lily's bones feel the same.
             She walks in the direction of the ocean.

ONE   She doesn't mind the rain, even the heavy
             rain.
             She takes off her shoes.
             And she walks down to a natural harbour and
             sits with her toes in the sand.
             Out on the ocean, she sees a boat.
             Smiles as it draws past.
             Except then it moves towards the shore.
             Like it's sheltering from the tempest, pushing
             closer and closer.
             She thinks, it can't be.
             But then the bow crunches the sand beneath it
             and out steps a woman.

The woman is old, her skin is leathered by
sun and sea salt.
Lily waves and the woman approaches.
The woman looks at this young girl, an adult
now, and sees echoes of herself.

GRAN   *I never thought I'd see you.*

LILY   *There's no house for you, there's no lavish
                meal, no tea, not yet.*

GRAN   *It's okay. We'll find somewhere.*

ONE   They smile, then – hand in hand – they head
                back to the boat.
                The pair cast off and drift over the horizon.

                And that's the end.

                *

A Nick Hern Book

A Sudden Violent Burst of Rain first published in Great Britain in 2022 as a paperback original by Nick Hern Books Limited, The Glasshouse, 49a Goldhawk Road, London W12 8QP, in association with Paines Plough, Rose Theatre and the Gate Theatre

Cover photo: Rebecca Need-Menear; design: Conor Jatter

Designed and typeset by Nick Hern Books, London
Printed in the UK by Mimeo Ltd, Huntingdon, Cambridgeshire PE29 6XX

A CIP catalogue record for this book is available from the British Library

ISBN 978 1 83904 111 2

www.nickhernbooks.co.uk

facebook.com/nickhernbooks

twitter.com/nickhernbooks